provocations

provocations

poems
Alistair Bamford

images
**Nigel Bewley · Paul Bonomini
John Clarke · Jane Glennie
Lucy Kayne · Melissa Youell**

PECULIARITY PRESS

www.peculiaritypress.co.uk

ISBN 978-1-912384-21-1

This work first published 2025
Peculiarity Press, an imprint of Leigh & Glennie Ltd
Ascot, Berkshire, SL5 9EA. © Leigh & Glennie Ltd 2025

Text © Alistair Bamford, 2025

Cover image © Melissa Youell

Images © Nigel Bewley (pages 2, 4, 27, 28), Paul Bonomini (pages ii, 47, 64, 78, 79, 87, 102), John Clarke (pages vii, 24, 31, 44, 58, 62, 69), Jane Glennie (pages 8, 20–21, 36, 41, 52–53, 90, 94–95), Lucy Kayne (pages v, x, 13, 15, 48, 73, 98, 101)

Poetic licence: events described in these poems happened but details such as names, places, genders, conversations and events may have been changed. They are not to be taken as fact

Extended versions of 'Provocations (1): an introduction to poetry', 'Provocations (2): the making of poetry' and 'Provocations (3): the reception of poetry' first appeared in *Twelve Rivers* vol.15 issue 1, vol.15 issue 2 and vol.16 issue 1 (2024–25)

The moral right of the authors has been asserted in accordance with the Copyright Designs and Patents Act, 1998

All rights reserved. Without limiting the rights under copyright reserved above, no part of this publication may be reproduced, stored or introduced into a retrieval system, or transmitted, in any form or by any means (electronic, mechanical, photocopying, recording, or otherwise), without the prior written permission of the publisher and authors of this book

Book design by Jane Glennie. Typeset in Turnip

But lord it was only just words, words – they meant nothing in the world to him, I might just as well have whistled. Words realise nothing, vivify nothing to you, unless you have suffered in your own person the thing which the words try to describe …

… and as for the magician with the fiddlebow in his hand, who sits in the middle of a great orchestra with the ebbing and flowing tides of divine sound washing over him – why, certainly he is at work, if you wish to call it that, but lord, it's a sarcasm just the same.

Samuel Langhorne Clemens (Mark Twain)
A CONNECTICUT YANKEE IN
KING ARTHUR'S COURT

Contents

Reader — 1
january — 2
Aubade — 3
like, honey — 5
after history — 6
Weight loss — 7
Once — 9
ascension place burial ground, cambridge — 10
there is a bear — 11
Baggage — 12
picture — 13
Jane (1971–2003) — 14
o rose — 15
Tulips — 16
grouting — 17
Orange — 18
pillow talk — 19
Prayer meeting — 22
wreaths — 23
sea view (transformation) — 24
the memory of colour — 25
Variations on 'for instance' — 26

PROVOCATIONS
(1) an introduction to poetry — 29

Covehithe — 34
colour — 35
cinema (muswell hill) — 37
Cinema (Crouch End) — 38
A (m)oth(er)'s dust — 39
For Andrew Malkinson — 40
(Ignore Hamlet) — 42
february — 43
Parky — 44
the necessity of loss — 45
Gardener's Delight — 46
Cyclamen — 49

Toccata on 'So' — 50
50 quid — 51
setting seed — 54
Lahore — 55
Swallows — 56

PROVOCATIONS
(2) the making of poetry — 57

vienna — 63
in hand — 65
Last gifts — 66
the memory of things — 67
fiddle — 68
sweetheart — 70
George Crabbe — 71
ta langue — 72
Animal love song — 73
I want — 74
Tuesday afternoon — 75
photograph — 76
Abduction — 77
Good wood (wassail) — 80
Wren and robin (wassail) — 81
Seven coal-heart boys (wassail) — 82

PROVOCATIONS
(3) the reception of poetry — 83

Janee — 88
Ghosts — 91
Toccata on 'How' — 92
The card — 93
missing — 94
Autumn — 96
unicycling on cloud nine — 97
socks — 98
Toccata on 'When' — 99
about — 100

Reader

I wish we could be reversed, mirrored, or not
reflected but inside out so you could live
in my red insides, my viscera, and see me.

Then looking in the mirror – not a mirror
but something to do with memory, spiral,
shell-like – would be where you start, and I cease to be.

And we – you – would be giving a voice to the
silence of things like children, a growing tree,
a matter of breeze, and the blood and ebb of sea.

january

this cold weather
the boots can't dance,
the piano
is drained of riffs
and the white page
holds its ghosts tight

but oh how air,
the dust and air
sigh and sing as
inside cloud keys
and these white words
fat buds, green things,
good things grow right

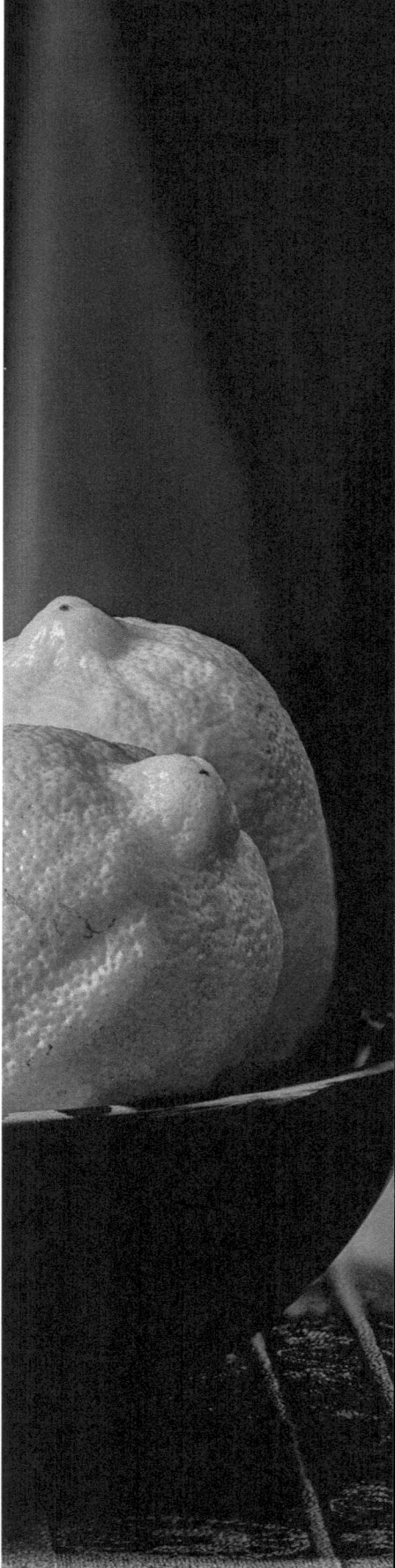

Aubade

There is a window past the foot of the bed,
in the wall opposite, as briefly soft as
only a face from sleep – apricot perfect,
a space of joy flushed sweet; and after, waking
again, merely an indeterminate grey.

The window will never be there again, not
that one gifted to Dear Reader and hanging
by a thread of eyesight (eyesigh the typo
said, which is cool). This morning's window, slightly
later, is soft Mondrian on the landing wall.

Reluctant to be seen from the slippered haul
towards the bathroom it wears its art lightly,
unaware, barely clocked on the bleary way for a
pee and poo and cleaning teeth first thing,
unwished into being, unmissed but not forgot.

Oh tomorrow's window, open into me,
in us, each green, blue, gold possibility
of rebirth, both daily and eternally;
and once past this fuss and forgot, let the
colours of the children continue to be.

like, honey

there is jigsaw-puzzle-in-a-charity-shop lady,
and dead-dog rose-lady, how these were small, quiet forms of love
and simple and innocent, and i bought a knackered leather
jacket and we will chat in passing and that's nice, that's nice

the magnolia grandiflora is superb but not simple,
after a quarter of a century the face in the coffin
still a complicated place to be, but it only
blossoms two, three, maybe four weeks a year so that's nice too

i cannot say joy because it only has three letters,
and joyful's a pathetic half-dozen, not the infinity
of sounds in the tongue, under the fingers, but this moment
is outside wars (plural four) which may change us in the twinkling

do not cry, sitting there your eyes black with sharp wet fruits –
you cannot know what that does to me but it does several things,
which you would like but that's not the point, that's not where we are,
don't cry. sit and talk – wipe those tears – there, that's nice, that's really nice

after history

ma from the new happy swan was the first to burn joss sticks,
in her ritual at the restaurant door, until dad did.
1966 and all that. wanting a flowery shirt

to salvage something kinder, more benign if less certain
from the fallen idols, lies, hypocrisies of v for
victory. the beatles remained hot, cool, whatnot. let it be

the space race, moon landing, leeds, revie, ali, munich, red rum,
oh man place a bet and despair at the collapse at becher's
of the tiny ozymandiae as silly schoolboys fight, fight

possibility, need, change, not revolution but more
nearly disdain for the folly of agreeing with those
who rule merely by being. let it be, let it be

to say not to know war is to repeat it, while to know war is
to watch while others repeat it. words of wisdom and all that

Weight loss

Jelly seemed to be for sweetness and memories,
katsu curry appetite and curiosity,
defying the dull vanilla thuds of protein shakes
and breaking teeth on biscuits with a cup of coffee.

Having now swept up ashes to ashes, dust to dust,
of an evening there is still denial of sitting not
saying much, telly on, thinking about supper while
mum gurned and murmured hopelessly that her teeth were shot.

Mother, father, skin-and-bone supposed-lover going to
hell in a hand-cart: the disparate mysteries of each
small history will slim to invisibility,
from simulacred triumphs to final loss of speech.

Hauling hard on the end of an old belt to try and
do it up, flattening still-thick fat, flesh, skin against still-
wet bones, this is all definitively what does and
does not happen as part of eating, breathing and being ill.

Once

Tall, dark hair tied back in a pony tail. Lately it became
grey and free and streaked as sea, clumped on shrunken yellow shore,
hospital gown open in unaware indignity.

Stood at the sink not so long ago – 'stood', but in truth reaching
up anxiously, fingers unhooked from rigor for a plate
from the rack, 'not so long ago' once more eight forever.

Sis said 'cremate her in her favourite clothes': tweed skirt and holey green
jumper, mail order or bought on some shopping trip way, way
before such things were reduced to memories and TV.

Cotton Traders, Coopers, and the shrunk pink sweatshirt that was red
once and belonged decades ago to me, become osmosed
through sporadic washes between weeding, gravy, dog.

In fact roughly the colour of the stains that stayed in her bedroom
carpet despite the efforts, the first time it happened, to scrub,
scrub, scrub against the gagging at mother's shit and blood.

A needingness persists, falling through the door from the clothing
companies, Laithwaites, Which?, the gardening and book catalogues,
unaware each cancellation cancels her some more.

ascension place burial ground, cambridge

he is remembered with a thick slip of greening stone
towards the far end of the burial ground, squeezed between
the incised aggrandisements of men but not women, wives'
names added to each in the space left, through thick grass, at the base.

declaration of war the week mark died aged nine, his loss
lost under the pyramids of men who didn't come back,
or did with bits blown off – uncle douglas lost a leg in
a tank (dad called him legless douglas but not, thank god, to his face).

ill, iller, illest – a declension of pre-war prep school lore
or billy bunter, jennings; not latin on a grey
monday morning, obscure doings of caecilius in
horto, pliny in pompeii, tacitus, amo amas –

mark was ill, iller, illest (memorised tomorrow
boys) and mum remembered how little tim came to stay
because douglas was away, until the day they had to
say, and tim asked for mark's trainset and ascended to his place.

they came back each year to visit and probably leave flowers,
until aunt's alzheimer's came into play and what with
one thing and another it was no longer practicable,
and so the thick slip of greening stone, and this page, become his grace.

there is a bear

in a dirty green jacket, bluey fleecy thing,
not so sure about the rest but it's a bear,
with bare feet. the joke would be better if it
was funny, not lying on the pavement by
heffers, opposite trinity, zero degrees.

in the bookshop they say 'ask them', with a point
across the road, so i do; and the porters
report 'sorry, nothing to do with us, call
the police, ambulance, but she won't thank you
for it'; so a young chap standing by does that.

her hair, unlike her language, isn't filthy,
not a thing you'd choose to sniff but soft, like clean,
like normal; asked again, the porters offer a
space blanket, which we wrap her in so she can
take it off again, repeatedly, while swearing.

reflected in heffers window we talk over
the 'fuck off' and 'bugger off' and 'i'll hit you'
and their echoes, the raising a mottled fist,
and reply 'ok darling, but put your shoes on
first', which being a bear that's drunk she can't do.

it's the foot, the bare feet, sandals a couple
of feet away (remember: zero degrees,
nearly Christmas, festive purple flesh, crowns of
horns on yellow toes) – 'don't want cuppa tea, fuck off',
chap gives a fiver for a filet-o-fish, 'i luv you'.

my mate sarah, who is not hokey, she says
we all need angels, so by the by where's my
gabriel? i need my own little things with wings
because darling bear i see, hear you in me, i
hear, see me in you, as echoes, and mirrors, and am scared.

Baggage

There is a large red suitcase in the loft, not yet full
but it's for you. Granny's wedding dress is in there, cleaned
and folded and packed like time in tissue, new tissue
(bless you) – if it hadn't existed neither would you.

Jewellery mostly was nicked that day the dog was
at the vet's but they missed a silver pendant, chips of diamond
and ruby outlining your age – how old now? – and a
few tiny boxes and little velvet bags like sighs.

There are some dollar bills, big ones; there are a few books
even though, like clothes (yes some of those), dads are told they
don't know what to buy; outgrown packed-up wrapped-up grown-up
debris from years of absence – and these are the mere thing-things.

I would give, if I could, the tseep-tseep-tseep of a small bird
in a big tree on the main road yesterday;
the tree itself, or the one draped in December sun
over the wall and higher than the house next door.

There should be forests for fires for warmth; incense to make
the dogs sing hymns; whisper it: in your quiet corner saints, angels, kings –
but this is all yoked with straps, nipped by the little jaws
of the case's zip, holding the whole lot fiercely in until …

… please, please, in return, after I've poked thin eyes through
a few pages of *Pickwick Papers* give me back the quiet sleep
night stole while I lay wide-eyed-shut, that missed the silver
pendant in my attic head, and the howl in my heart of raw red.

picture

a grubby rectangle above the radiator
where the picture hung – they will repaper, paint over
it sometime, it's just what happens after so many years.

the picture itself – foreground spiked by teasels, behind
them an estuary, blue sky, scraps of birds – is gone too,
sold to steve down the road who does antiques (nice price thank
you, already spent on mot, service, two new tyres).

letter sellotaped to the back shows the artist on
the make being chummy, dad on the make spending money,
and wishing-the-ground-would-swallow-her-up mummy.

should have copied it, as fabricated evidence
of a rare nice day, a positive negative, proof
of absence; and how without rectangles and pictures
the past – histories, facts, truth – is quickly wiped away.

Jane (1971–2003)

Looking through the same window each day: the sky this morning definitely
blue, gaining green from the sun's dropping, slightest left-light of trees,
    flower beds, hedge.

Those days of talking, thinking, playing the violin, and saying again;
then these days the tinny echoes of easy intensities and joys – here: gone.

Say, if you can, why we are neither here nor gone, sky neither blue nor green
but bruised grey. Let's discuss it briefly before turning away for a drink.

Cheers and all that to the crass making light of coming night that returns
daily, again, more often than can in any conceivable universe be right.

And after the rain there is a purl of traffic noise, hiss of tyres, growl of
a lorry, bus on the hill, same as usual, taking up the reins of the mundane.

o rose

a red flower floating in a white bowl

this is the neutral way to describe

how tears extinguish a burning body

this is the neutral way to describe

the darker places placed behind veils

this is the neutral way to describe

where lambs are eaten and a star explodes

this is the neutral way to describe

not how things were but how they come to be

this is the neutral way to describe

a red flower floating in a white bowl

Tulips

i
The bulbs were a gift, and became spectacular in their pomp:
great bleeding fists, piratical bruised hearts and wide emptied eyes.

But times changed as they became ours over years, and us was gone
to dust and fuck that, and the question becomes: who owns beauty?

ii
And if they are dug up now, suppose the unearthed engorged balls
of future delights burst out into another unknowing Spring?

Make no allowance for beauty's due, no allowance that he
loved her but she was never adored, which she begrudged.

iii
The trowel is a feeble lever into and under the fat
roots of triumphant Agapanthus they were planted among.

The trowel is like a Stanley knife to slice not just fist, heart and eye
but daddy, daddy, and plump brown bulbs that next door's tabby shat.

grouting

i
the grouting still isn't finished because thursday five years ago,
after the en suite was done, she flips back the duvet and lies there
in an inelegant way, a thin lady croaking her vague 'thank you'

while mum was in hospital having shat and bled all over her
bedroom floor – friday, someone needs to go and clean up or social
services will say she can't cope, and that would finish her off

he says ' i've got to go' and she says 'no or that's it' and he goes
(you would), and after three days with no sleeping, waking or dying
it's (it turns out planned, not mum but) all over bar the shouting

the trigger, the key, is either sheer laziness (possible) or
ptsd (also possible) from the days and years after monday:
to grout, like everything else, gives time to think, feel and doubt

ii
hand, wrist, arm pump up and down like billy-o
but this is not a wank more's the pity but
scrubbing the newly tiled wall clean of dried grout,
and the doctor's best offer is 'tennis elbow'.

it's all sore and aches to buggery, and this
is definitely contrary to the climactic
and more like second cousin to something like
housemaid's knee, which in a manly sense is a swizz.

but at last there is a tremble on the brink of
coming to a stop because it hurts so much,
the tiling's done and this is how it ends, not
butch but fluffing diy into a public cough.

Orange

i
The great three of satsuma, sofa and tree
don't naturally seem to go together
in one breath but that's how, here, they choose to be.

Fruit and tree – tree burnished by sunslip light, seen
driving (me, not the tree) home over the brow of
the hill – are relatively OK partners.

I give sweet segments of one to the parrot
to wet his beak and cheer him up; the other's
unexpected glory gave itself to me.

ii
I say 'this isn't going anywhere' and
'I've had enough' and make to walk away, past
the orange sofa standing near the door.

And I'm a big bloke, big enough so when
she steps in front and says 'where are you going,
you're just trying to control things as usual', I shrug.

I say 'excuse me', step round and walk by, a
slight stumble in front of the sofa as, some haunted
spirit of a Knight of Ni, she shoves me.

iii
Don't deny the glory days but all there is to
do is, as Mum said and as I've done, as you would
be done by, and forget sofa, fruit and sun.

pillow talk

though these are words whereas
what is remembered
still, after years, are those
deeds and deed the day,
the evening, street light,
touch, and blue good night

rest a remembered head
here, or here, with no
matter where or how those
curled strands are strewd, as
long as such sweet stilled heads
still make deep, deep dents

arranging, plumping up
the pillows, always
in the end plumping for
the same ones, with the
lumpy others still being
plumped as though for two

Cup**ss**.

Wilderness.

MISS.

CARR

Prayer meeting

The pub has a back room, and Monday lunchtime is quiet anyway.
Having been gone so long from each other there is nothing particular but on the other hand anything, everything, to say.

No conversation beforehand about food – whether to eat, or just coffee, or spend the day.
Or whether this is a big deal, or just some slightly happy chance to catch up without an emotional price to pay.

And then the time has gone, having covered the usual bases of what's in the news, people, places, work, play.
And the time comes to call it a day and go separate ways with memories intact, muttered pangs and no more scope to betray.

In the olden days but no more – 'you make your bed' is what mum said – people used to stay.
Dad drank like a fish, lashed out, dressed up, swore vehemently he wasn't gay.

The wrong choice was leaving in that watery sun to make some hay.
Forgive these cheap unhelpful rhymes: to pray in black and white leaves only grey.

wreaths

please don't try spinning the line that it's a pagan or earth-mummy thingy,
and get off my tits about sacrilege and bad language: mum was a mary
too, and it must have been as rosy in the birth canal then as today

the last one i was involved with we clubbed together – sister, brother, me –
yellow and white flowers in green she mightn't have liked much but history
is full of the games you have to play, and the cost was ok between three

what does feel a little odd though, not quite ok, is workshops for making the
darned things these days, seemingly everyone getting it on with some holly,
tinsel and ribbon to mark the birth and therefore death of a bloody baby

sea view (transformation)

they said the earth is flat and if you go too far you will fall off the edge, or perhaps there was a look-out, or people only fell off after dark. there's a chap with a torch called the strawberry moon, who colours the sea in bands up to a line of eyebrow pencil, and we kneel on a turquoise sofa at the tall first floor window. a small black dog says 'love me, love me doo-be-doo' because if you cannot jump high enough you will fall in the sea, and the world will turn out not to be round after all.

the memory of colour

coming out of a canadian winter (they called it spring
but you wouldn't know it) two days after the wedding,
freezing rain, she asks him, road becoming covered in snow
over the ridge (she asked me) to drive her dad's two-tone bronco

landing at heathrow with grass bottle-green as, well, a bottle
by the runway, and skies trying to be tropical,
and cherry blossom flying flights of honour on the link
road, A3 into town, of the tartiest fuck-off pink

those were bright, bright colour days – not quite that the rest
have quite faded (that's middle age for you) or they will be best
ever (but maybe) but they were simply gobsmacking
in their, in such spectacular innocent fandangoing

so drag back from oblivion, out of the oblivious,
the blossom and the bottle-green grass and leaves, the curious
impertinent fingers of daffodils down the lane,
and the mild pallors of intimate pelts forgetting pain

Variations on 'for instance'

na przyklad tying balloons on the door handles of
ambulances is worth so much more than empty words

par exemple to stop on a dog walk and to look
across the water meadows and it feels calm and green

zum beispiel there are rhymes like tunes and spoons and june's
but it's too tough to make very much out of these

por ejemplo he asks himself whether they could boost
the input portals of an inflatable doll, but doubts it

till exempel here is another drawing of an
owl in a tree, or a tree from which the owl has flown

per esempio oh earth mother, oh mother earth,
we are the flat-hand slap of mankind on your soft cheek

ealaa sabil almithal he might stroke his beard and
calculate the trajectory-to-impact ratios

lemashial there is another owl, not the tree one
but still a wise one who i think knows how real life works

er enghraifft the white-haired man has seen war and knows
it brings peace only to those who live in palaces

naprimer the little girl who is now grown up gives
her a kiss and says 'love you mum, see you very soon'

for instance mum tucks a yorkie in a stocking top,
rolls up bright sleeves and drives it across Europe

provocations
(1) an introduction to poetry

I

Poetry is Not Prose, although it can be. Sorted.

II

Poetry links gesture, sound and mark-making. Gesture suggests intention – it is about something – and invites reaction. Sound replicates, refines and transmits gesture. Gesture and sound are preserved and communicated through mark-making – writing.

Gesture, sound and mark-making together allow the creation and transmission of culture. At its broadest this is the acceptance and expression of common space and knowledge. Within the concept of culture poetry invites the prioritising of feeling over fact. In so doing it gives a momentum to uncertainty as well as certainty, and the implied and the liminal as well as the absolute. It might even be a way to describe the indescribable.

III

Poetry has roots in the insistency of walking and talking, and how as a species and as children we have learned to do these things. In this sense it perhaps predates prose. As a conscious artform the earliest forms of poetry were spoken as structured, heightened and thereby ritualised sound. Sound is transient and mutable whereas ritual – rhythm and repetition, rhyme, pitch and contour – anchors it.

Marks turn sound into memory by documenting it. Hieroglyphic and other writing systems may retain an essence of image but the journey of writing has been towards abstraction, through representing the component sounds that describe an object rather than being pictographic representations of it. The structures of language – the orthographies – then allow a shared understanding of the spoken and the written.

There is an inherent complementarity between spoken and written language – they refer to each other. There are also, arguably, neurological implications – brain rewiring – that are a consequence of the control that writing allows. This includes a shift from orality to literacy and also, again arguably, from a female- to a male-centred hegemony, and a related control and thereby determination of history, information and technology.

IV

How do animals communicate, and what are the implications for the richer modes of communication humans might claim for themselves (ourselves)? I taught my dog to read (sit/heel/down etc rather than Shakespeare but

he would have got there in the end, bookcase by his bed). On the whole he seemed happy eating, running, smelling (both sniffing and rolling-in) and sleeping – getting treats for reading was a bonus.

The key thing isn't the fact of something but the intention behind it, and in this case it was (unintentionally) classic hegemonic control over my dog (sorry Charlie). His poetry was in essence instinct – he never (as far as I know) felt a need to control information by writing things down. Here's a thing: children are bribed to develop the means to conform. Teaching children to read doesn't make them more human, just more like our version of human – but it also liberates them to be more fully themselves. Paradox is a handy thing.

V

Language and its extensions can be manipulative, from intimate seduction or the bribery inherent in capitalism, by way of the charismatic speaker to (looking in one direction) the claims of politicians and conspiracy theorists and (looking in another) the frogmarch of AI – but where would we be without it? Well we couldn't express doubts or ask questions, in which case we are doomed to be classically hegemonically controlled. Who by? Ah, there's a story – possibly the orangutan with the biggest weapons.

Sidestepping poetical prose, perhaps prose tends to tell whereas poetry implies. It offers a silly little safe space where we can doubt and ask questions, albeit often posited through answers (look at Keats's 'To Autumn'). We ask and find them as writers, and we ask and find them as readers and listeners.

VI

If prose proposes facts ('bear coming'), it tilts towards poetry by adding succinct feelings ('afraid of bear from last time' – hear the tremor in the voice), and memory projected into the future ('hope I'm not afraid of bear next time'). In other words poetry gives us time – a present (bear), a past (last bear) and a future (next bear). 'Emotion recollected in tranquillity' (Wordsworth) and all that. Bear with me.

Poetry takes supposed facts beyond the factual. It ('smells like teen spirit…') happens on two value-planes, one aural (rhythm, rhyme, assonance, pitch and so on) and one emotional (it makes me feel thingy). Such comments contain their opposites or inversions: the prosaic ('mind the gap') can be poetic, and the poetic (greetings cards?) can be prosaic.

This is important: poetry is not about how it is written but how it is read (which can directly contradict the writer's intention). It is about understanding through listening and reflection, not the imposition of an agenda. If an agenda is imposed then the reader is reading their own prejudice, not the poem. Don't reverse-engineer someone writing about murder into a murderer.

Consider censorship, threats to writers and publishers, book-burning, pulling down statues. Whether these things are right or wrong, they have happened. To commit a small act is to condone a large one, but if bad things are done by good people it begs the question not 'what' but 'why'. Such acts elevate writing from the mundane to the political. We are what we do, not what we write, but then to write becomes to do, understand and forgive.

VII

The greetings card thing straddles poetic and anti-poetic. My mother had a tight-lipped determination to say, when he died, that my father loved us. Here's a challenge, to write an expressive limerick: 'There is an old man who is deady / Who kept all his love in his heady. / He may have tried hard / But he kept his mouth barred / From admitting his heart wasn't ready.'

Technological change may pretend to bridge the chasm between high art (for which read 'establishment', 'middle class', 'privilege' and so on, which I'm afraid is largely what we're talking about here) and the demotic ('ordinary', 'normal', 'down the pub', limericks etc.) Here's a contentious suggestion: setting aside the issue (and it's a big one) of ownership of the data used to train AI, it's OK to like AI-generated poetry if we like it. Spot the difference. The real issue is our capacity to write, read and listen with our own hands, eyes and ears.

What we are all actually doing is – life consists of – filling the time between waking and sleeping, and birth and death. Poetry offers the occasional punctuation point because it is easier to focus on presence (look at this) than absence (silence) as it invites communion – reflection, argument, stimulation, confrontation, desolation, catharsis – along the way.

Covehithe

Threads coming to a skull on the shore:
line of golden-mountained cloud stapled
by three distant ships away beyond the
brown waves' run, run, run, run to the land.

The road to here has been uncertain through
winter fields and trees, bodach peering
through a run, run, run of rain on windscreen
as our cliffs sough softly into sand.

There are few myths left about old men
but we will run, run with sticks and frames
while woods decay and wizened roots pull
us down in the spume and waves come still.

And suns and moons will run this eastern sea
through each day's momento mori of
withdrawing roar, unheard by hollow
ships and bones beneath each brown wave's hill.

colour

oxbloods, sta-prest, braces, harrington
over sharp white button-down ben sherman

two kids going home from granny's, scared
by a pair of tractor boys on the train

norman and the bits of piss are long
in the land of bald old shits, but it stays

also: cotton pants stuck through with
mottled sticks of thighs all shades of greys

blessedly, before dark, a girl in
specsavers, dms patent sunset pink

fantasies don't cut it this christmas –
all those festive failures to feel and think

try black, white, green, red triangle, blue
river, six-pointed star, muslim, jew

List of Books. J.B. 1851

No	Name		Name
1	Latin Dictionary		Dr Scales Eng & Lat
3	Latin Testament		Eutropi[us]
	French		Ditto
	[illegible] French		Goldsmith
			Bible

cinema (muswell hill)

jungle book, on the buses – mummy said 'you can't go'
to saturday morning pictures with angharad phillips
'because I say so', despite her valentine: still don't know

why she couldn't be mine. *close encounters* with sarah though no
cigar and no corn was popped. odeon – now everyman –
love-seats in wipe-clean leatherette – oo missis, miss, oh

mrs fairfax-jones: how we groaned and saw *fitzcarraldo*,
macbeth, *tess* twice at hampstead just in case she was on duty
to witness her wicked husband trounced by a teenage hero

mythologizing lust. albinoni adagio,
shostakovitch on the soundtrack to *rollerball*-broken
victor, a mere survivor now, superman to zero,

smaller than ever before: and how to tell whether to
return, or even just to recall, is ok. abc, sticky
carpet, 'you'd adore a kia ora', fleapit, xyz. finito.

*A suburban upbringing is bounded by cinemas – here from
the Odeon (now Everyman) Muswell Hill, by way of Swiss
Cottage and Tottenham Court Road back to the long-gone
ABC. Mrs Fairfax Jones was an art teacher whose husband
owned the original Everyman Hampstead.*

Cinema (Crouch End)

In the bitter hinterland between the burgeoning and the railway,
the behinds of the unwealthy sought sagged webbing and
    much-rubbed bouclé.
Before (and before tea) words of worth had made vague shrifts
    round these red bricks,
which then were hymned and censed by chokes of blue smoke
    from cars blokes couldn't fix.

Following God, and crap sofas, and third-hand motors with a guarantee
to go for years that went for scrap, and leaking roofs and rats
    and stink of pee,
the Sally Army is replaced by march of beards and weed and film, and nous
to resurrect debased and broken sacred into secular art house.

Now Man is worshippéd and glorified on red plush seats in Dolby,
with Pearl & Dean and previews, craft beers, brownies, single estate coffee;
and queues form left and right for tickets, loos, and quiet foods
    to chew between
the request to silence phones, and horror-stricken hush at what has been.

Testament to follicles and what accountants called financial madness,
bless you for the film, and for Sassoon, for soldiers, love and
    death and sadness.

Now hipster heaven, Crouch End used to be on the run-down periphery of North London complete with places of worship repurposed as warehouses and workshops. Poet Siegfried Sassoon is the subject of the film Benediction.

A (m)oth(er)'s dust

i
There was to be a dark mark by the plughole in
 the sink, size of a coin: a moth, nipped on the wing
between thumb and finger, leaving a damp grey must.

ii
Scraping old paint makes a powder that scours the eyes.

Grains of seeming sand, tipped from a cheap pot into a
hole in the ground: Mum has become a familiar loss,
but not the dry tension of her dust cupped in the hand.

Decorating, mother, tune tight across the chest.

iii
Other: the heft, shape, moth of a Vulcan bomber
photo'd on the back wall of a museum display.
Do you know the size of a ball turret on a
B-17? Not the Moms in Idaho, in
Illinois, whose boys wrote 'Back soon, tell Gracie 'hi' ',
and rose repeatedly from the concrete runes.

iv
Ball turret gunner Jonny and his buddies bailed out over
Regensburg, phoenixes assways-round as balled-up socks.

This tightness gets under the nails, under the skin.

For Andrew Malkinson

||: ...this is not about the bollocks of poetry but
something for which we all have responsibility –
personally, institutionally.

I don't know the facts, this is not my story, but it
could have happened to me or you. Fuck the 'balance of
probability' and do not refuse your empathy: the
innocent by definition are not the guilty.

As he said this morning (Mr Malkinson please
forgive me): '...police, prison officers, probation,
prisoners, journalists, judges... As a minority
of one you are forced to live their false fantasy.'

Sure, ask how I would feel if something bad happened to
someone close to me: I can't be sure of my reply.
But logically bad deeds cannot be healed by
the blood-letting needs of society.

In return let me ask you about mendacity,
mediocrity, the conveniently lazy, not
as vague concepts but as tool, lock and key that for... :||

...seventeen years cancelled his liberty.

Found innocent
||: :|| = *repeat this section ad libitum*

(Ignore Hamlet)

To be a Man is (ignore Hamlet) simply to Be.

There is no mechanism, not really, for working
out, fine-tuning an updated, liberated 'He',
just the questionable descent from and descant to
intercourse, the womb, at the birth, Earth Mother, Queen Bee.

To be a Man is (ignore Hamlet) simply to Be.

To leave merely the same stains in the same places – pants,
bog, bolus in hanky, bottom of the sea, moon, soon Mars
('sorry, s'orright mate, bantz, carried away') – and cast around
like a frightened dog ('let me out') needing somewhere to pee.

To be a Man is (ignore Hamlet) simply to Be.

Mansplaining and silence apart from the odd (better believe
it: odd) irresistible fart. 'That's not what', says She,
 'you mean'. He who dealt it painted the bathroom green. 'All
you need is Love' – oops, and Fairy Tales – oops, and Honesty.

To be a Man is (ignore Hamlet) simply to Be.

There's shits who know what's what, what/who they're up to,
duck, dive and on the hoof (the bed) – but on the whole unknowingly.
Tongues prised from cheeks, ignominies and private parts, Hear Ye
with Love and Honesty and (oops, ignoring Hamlet) simply Be.

february

i
in the old calendar (we are talking ancient)
this day didn't exist, suspended outside planting
and harvesting, outside the beginning and the end

and then green comes and resurrection is invented
and time's awkward orthography, clunky as fuck,
becomes incised on lives, city walls and valentines

ii
i would call you a runt for your underwhelming puny
echoes of the great empires of the year, but we are
reborn together (a dead man said 'semblable') each day

we mewl wide-eyed and -mouthed, safe in the palaces
we know from the devastations on the radio
and our cosy hypocrisies carved in black and white

iii
so unprick prophylaxis, that grey-lipped madonna thing,
the frottage of man/woman, right/wrong, good/evil
and all the routine, vulgar, lazy, cheap assumptions

all I want – too much? – is a smidge of green against the
(another dead man said) dying of the light – just let me,
let me sleep a little longer, and then plant lavender

Parky

Nothing personal of course, just a national thing
beginning with headlines on the telly one morning.
No baggage, love child, Jimmy here to be fixed upon
an altar of hypocrisy ('now then') – ey-oop, he's gone.

And the body will be popped safely out of the way
so's not to interfere with TV clips from his heyday,
the band will play his theme tune on the heavenly stage,
and we're reminded of his charm but not of his great age.

the necessity of loss

acts that sprinted yelling through playgrounds,
decorated houses and buried a
mother muddle dna and law,
manipulation and the economy

to remember is last year's milk (with
january long gone), insects caught
fleetingly in cupped hands, images and
words just wind and dust and electricity

there is a surprising, a preening
self-satisfaction in such anger,
fear, vulnerability: to threaten
to grow – and to grow – bigger than honesty

the journeys round the eyes amaze, routes
crêped without abyss from birth to nearly
sleep, just hollowness scoured by and from
the sand and rocks of forgotten secret facts

Gardener's Delight

18 strawberry plants at some complicated discount
per strip, and tomato, courgette, cucumber seeds
plus herb seeds and potting compost and four growbags,
that together add up to a surprising amount.

Creation, that's how it will have started, God down
the garden centre for earlies and onion sets, a
ficus of necessity for birthday suits, and
birthday cards for next door's gods in next door galaxies.

Need the loo pronto, café for a scone, and seek
help to load the Honda Jazz ('only five years old,
retirement present to Self, can't spend it when you're
gone'), scoff pills and creak past vintage towards antique.

From dust to dust, portentous as heck, in drills
they bud and leaf and leave, with stains and inch on lips,
guts, hips from votive-hearted sugar-fisted fruits,
the drive home ashed by vergent shouts of golden daffodils.

Cyclamen

A corm – just the one – lifted
from the clay soil, breathed, teased with
the tip of a broken trowel
the last time leaving mum's, then
left with other bits of plant
in a black bin bag until
three days later, yellowing,
they did all get planted out.

Planted, buried under the
weeping ash where the doves sit
and do what they do on the car
and then coo, pretending all
innocence – no, they are not,
they know perfectly well what
they do, they do it on purpose.

The builders have since been back
and forth for months, mini-digger,
things buried, forth and back and
anyway the point is there
is no memory any
more, except this quiet nailing
of plant to poetry.

Toccata on 'So'

So there is a knock on the door (there never was a bell).
So she answers it and he says 'Can I come in' and she says 'It's your house' and he comes in, with a frankly rude woman in tow.
So she says 'I am asking you not to remove anything today without agreement except personal things' (although he will) and goes back into the kitchen.
So there is another knock on the door and there is her friend for moral support, plus the removals men to price it up.
So her friend is in the kitchen now while he and the rude woman make occasional bangs and thumps around the house.
So after a while she makes tea for the visitors and for the removals men when they put their heads round the door, boiling a small saucepan of water as the kettle was taken before.
So after another while he comes into the kitchen and says 'I see you haven't made me any tea, can I have a glass of water please?'
So she says 'Of course you can, you know where the glasses live'.
So he takes one from the cupboard over to the sink and reaches for the tap.
So she says 'Oh, can you put 5p on the side please' and he says 'I'm sorry?' and she says 'Can you put 5p on the side, for the water, I'm paying the bill'.
So he turns from the sink and takes two or three steps towards her, raising the hand holding the glass.
So at the moment he lets go of the glass a look on his face seems to say 'Oh no' as if to pull him back from the brink but it is too late as it smashes at her feet.
So the shards fan under the table and across the floor to the far wall under the radiator and the fridge.
So he says 'It slipped, I'll sweep it up' and goes towards the cupboard where the dustpan and brush live.
So she says 'No, you know it didn't' and 'I think it's time for you to go'.

50 quid

What a pleasure, what a barn-storming fucking pleasure
to put his own food, bought with his own money, in his
own little fridge got second-hand from round the corner.

Wondered whether to haggle for it or to maintain
a middle-aged diffidence, not least as the type who
would not push her off, not even when she bit his face.

Never liked that tight violence of twisting nipples
between knuckles – not his price for the cheap white joy
it brought, the making of a thin milk of humanity.

Bloke outside the charity shop shouting, and it's drugs
or drink or some such: makes him flinch again, lost with a
map of lies and then, abused, left nowhere else to hide.

It was cold outside but clearly not cold enough, and
the milk poured in chunks and was not nice. See now, too late,
how things can of necessity be kinder both in tea and life.

setting seed

rather than buying a bunch of flowers he picks a large thistle (carefully),
some little yellow thingies, and they are stood good as gold in
    a blue glass vase

at it last night and knackered and to be fair she's totally there but now
what a bloody fuss – all he done was ('scuse me) hoick up his prick
    and scratch his arse

pat on bum, sat down to eat, and she bristles. they was out of bouquets down
the garidge he said, as he shoved the bunch of weeds (and they stink)
    in the vase

morning, sore head and thighs, she finds the seed heads have exploded into bits
of kittens, puppies, teddy's stuffing. he laughs: wha's wrong? hangover my arse!

she saw something like these seeds once before, image in the paper of the
love-child of a sputnik and a spider's web, imagined among the stars

momentarily mum before grasping handfuls of plant fluff for the bin bag,
she was once herself a few atoms spun somewhere in a venus full of mars

feet up out the way till she's ready to come down but she's off on one, off
with the fairies about mess, spunk-nits, looney cycles, bollocks about stars

planets roll from shores of kohl still there from last night's jink as flowers fucked,
vase emptied, sighs at the sink, hand on tum, she's now herself a venus full of mars

Lahore

Oh Whitechapel, Commercial Road, Brick Lane (before it
got posh): not chicken shop nor flock-walled restaurant but
the nearest formica'd curry house is where we'd go.

Every other night it seemed, less than eight quid eats and
they wasn't licensed but BYOBs which we did,
gaggled round a table and chutneyed nineteen to zero.

Not York Hall boxing (never been) but lunchtime strippers
Bethnal Green (Salmon & Ball, quid in the jar, don't touch),
those was the days etceterar: gone, centuries ago.

Jack the Chipper, Blind Beggar, traders, wankers, tarts (not
me); weeds, hoardings, peeling walls, pee up walls, sirens,
Royal London, lookin' for blood, finding Tesco Metro.

Staggered through the whitening morn to the bagel shop top
of Brick Lane, as one more Sunday wrang detritus from the night
before, and down Columbia Road the flowers flow.

Swallows

In late middle age there is a slow migration south,
as an almost mythical kettle of swallows follows
the well-worn wings of antecedents, hatched by parents
to stuff lies in each engorging yellow-caverned mouth.

The gut is swollen now, distended past anything
that could somehow take wing, round which this thick belt constrains,
becomes equatorial; and photos have become
memorials at which fat men are too late to sing.

If at one time the swallows made summers, then such fun
melded into a season of slow, thick lying on the
earth; of rollings, rather than skyward interweaved and
joyous wheelings, where untimely passings have begun.

Swallows are Full English Breakfasts, lap-top suppers, nine
pints that night down the pub, and all dragged down the gullet
day-in, day-out, displacing taut gut with belly fat,
tight as a drum designed to beat all to the end of time.

Friends, my friends, you too will fly from uterus to red-
walled crematoria, and unresolved rituals
of scattering handfuls of ashes in dry proxy
for laughter, mucking about and your cold bed.

provocations

(2) the making of poetry

I

What to write about. How to write about it. Who it's written for. Blank paper or screen, and a vague unease or urgency. I wanna hold your hand (and you to hold mine).

II

Let's park who a poem is written for, beyond saying it may well be written for the writer. It may be the writer getting some personal rocks off, or perhaps something is clamouring to be shared – an experience, a perception, an anger, perhaps expressed by way of some mellifluous or punchy hook or phrase – probably rocks and clamour and that's OK.

Would the world be worse off without poetry? Possibly not, but that's not the point. The world is only fractionally better with Bach and table tennis and finding 10p on the pavement but those are all, on balance, gains.
The brilliant thing about poetry is that it is quick and cheap to make and consume – often more gourmet hot dog than the complete Mr Creosote but don't underestimate the power of pickles. And incidentally this paragraph assumes we have a shared, a cultural knowledge that embraces both Bach and Mr Creosote.

III

The writer needs a voice, and something to write about or to say – a sensibility. Within this there are things like 'vision', 'ability', 'self-belief' and 'pig-headedness', but the best word to describe the making of poetry may be simply 'courage' – the courage to make something from nothing, from the blank page and the miasma of things and thoughts and feelings and sounds that otherwise merely pass through us. With poetry you can have, eat, digest and excrete your cake – alimentary my dear.

Whether lived experience translates directly into written experience is debatable, but the act of writing responsibly through turning sensibility into an intentional thing (the poem) transmutes experience into art. A poem may be about all sorts of things but one of those things should be itself, the work. A person is not a poem and vice versa, and neither should be judged by the other.

IV

The builder has given me a parrot. That's a different story: the issue here is anxiety about what it may learn to mimic (there are things a little green lump of fluff shouldn't say). This raises the issue of imitation, which is predicated on pre-existing patterns. These patterns are the tropes of language whether written or heard, as the accumulation of sound by way of letters into word.

Language is inherently imitative – it is based on what we already know, or we wouldn't understand it. We understand language because of the number of times we have heard it, compounded by the emotions projected through it. Like parrot and egg, whether language or emotion comes first is an open question – probably, it depends on context. Anyway: poetry riffs on this implicit knowledge of language. It exists in and hopefully gives value to the space beyond imitation. It lies (and tells truths) in what is not imitation.

V

It is hearing (not necessarily the same thing as listening) that gives the poet a voice, and elevates poetry above the prosaic. It is hearing that gives voice to word choices, punctuation, rhythm, line lengths and breaks, strong and weak beats, delayed resolutions (rap is brilliant) and extended structural concerns.

Gerard Manley Hopkins is a great poet of sound, of trusting sound, and pushing it towards music while remaining in touch with a word-world. Trust: there's another element in the making of poetry – trust that it works, and that the reader/hearer will recognise that it works.

VI

Returning to sensibility, does the world need another poem about trees, autumn, or parenthood? Strictly speaking it may not, but such poems refresh if not renew the world. Where is the meeting place between trees, autumn and parenthood? I like the idea of the kaleidoscope, which when turned turns the same elements into new patterns. And for goodness sake, the world keeps changing (while staying the same), and so a poem may express change, or cling desperately to the seemingly familiar and safe. The possibility that nothing changes may itself be radical.

A lovely writer said 'I don't know what to write about if I don't write about my childhood'. It astonishes me that within the lifetimes of people I knew there was not only no broadband but no telly, planes or world wars. For goodness' sake: Great Granny was a girl in the early days of the bicycle. And people were being killed then, and they still are.

There is an issue of scale, of the intimate or domestic or personal in contrast with the grand and universal, but poetry can contain both within the same image. A baby is the world in waiting, autumn is the approach of death, and trees are – well, trees are just brilliant, but they also model the seasons and renewal and strength and patience, with bark but (unlike the parrot) no bite.

VII

An experience or perspective revealed through a poem – by Emily Dickinson say, or Sylvia Plath – gives the reader permission to acknowledge their own experience or perspective. Something may be expressed with an acuity that validates something we have known but haven't voiced, or it may shock with its strangeness. It may be harder sometimes to work out what that knowledge actually is, but maybe that's a poem thing, that apparent knowledge refuses to crystallise.

Waves breaking on the shore may be inherently poetic (or not and can we get back in the car please I'm bloody freezing and I want a cup of tea), but to describe them doesn't in itself make a poem. Incidentally waves-breaking-on-shore poems face some fierce competition (Tennyson, Matthew Arnold ... What did Mrs Arnold say, on honeymoon with Matty in that hotel room in Dover?) Try active writing and reading: what is a poem about?
No, what is it about?

A little provocation: that a work of art should be a safe space, safe from harm or harming, and safe to be radical. There shouldn't be things that are beyond the pale. Writing something sexy is only pornographic if the reader chooses to read it that way – whose rocks are being got off? If you don't like it, don't look now – but we must look now to talk about difficult and necessary things. Again: the work is not the person any more than 'Dover Beach' is about Mr and Mrs A snuggling down. Perhaps a poem is an actor, with a right and need to perform. It's hard to generalise but hey: sticks and stones. A poem doesn't kill.

vienna

there will still be castles and cakes – 'schloss', 'torte' she
   taught me, sitting on the steps, adding kissing

that lasted (with a break when she met a monk, long story, i
   met her mum, ditto, wink) years

where viennetta sliced from its wrapper round her house for
   tea didn't do it for me

never mind anschluss or strauss (my mum was six, liked the
   third man, taught me one weekend how to waltz)

but send us a card when you're there, and spare a thought for
   roly who popped his clogs recently

and his missus who never knew any of this, or the party
   where he shagged her (a different 'she')

while i was with the horn player who wore a black velvet
   ribbon round her neck and not much more

last day on tour, in the mountains, a pic of him sitting
   (unusually) on the fence

sun streaming through blonde hair become long gone forty-
   plus years on: git and angel and git again

to drink pints with, listen to led zeppelin, pollini, who briefly
   that morning anyone would have adored

in hand

i

tiny flutter of a bird held in the hand,
heart nineteen to the dozen in a gentle
cage of cupped fingers (so far, so fluffy)

and we, in turn, are birds in the fingers
of a whale (stay with me), held just as gently
(it's all relative) as ex and divorcee

but the (shut it jonah) the whale is held in turn
by some god, some universe unconcerned with
anthropomorphising and cute: which just 'is'

ii

so the bird (it's a parrot) says: 'i'll do you
a deal, smile' (they do), 'say your words, eat millet',
while the whale (it's a blues whale) sings 'where's my krilllll?'

and dry oceans, burnt forests, black skies fall silent
as the graves not just of ahabs but of answers,
of questions and of lives, where none embrace

Last gifts

The bodies were all but a miracle, never having seen them still before,
dad with a ruffle round his neck, mum in the dog-walking clothes
    she often wore.
The ruffle was a kind of coy hiding of the autopsy's goodness knows what;
mum was more natural, but with legs bandaged where they had
    started to rot.

Other stuff had been nicer – routine tat like socks and hankies; a pen, cash;
a microscope, Lego, Meccano; some books taken from big brother's stash.
Unless it was chucked there is still a watch at the back of a drawer,
    missing its ticks;
there are twenty eight more pieces of silver somewhere to go with
    the candlesticks.

A puppy widdles with excitement on a hot water bottle on a chair,
small and gorgeous and fluffy and, like the old phone number,
    no longer there.
Socks filled with holes, hankies snot, pens ran out of ink or were lost,
    dosh is long gone.
Never mind the abuses of time and love, just switch the bloody light on.

the memory of things

three of them – blue, white, green – jammed inside each other,
bag of peat on top, electric chainsaw perched on that
in a random marriage of mess. chainsaw set carefully
aside; hoicking up, plomping down the bag, it forgets
its neat compression and becomes fat; tubs to carry
logs in, winter coming, let them dry a bit, their cleaved
angles betraying ash tree until (bless you) ash time:
easier to say how things are than what they may mean.

this will be whispered once, and you must promise not
to tell (unlike those who lie too well and will burn to
ash in hell): the white tub has split with plastic fatigue.
grubby now with memory we (the blue and green will
say) were once unprised, clean for ice for not champagne but
even so something for a wedding – a sparkling bordeaux maybe.

fiddle

teasing racks of pale-banded close-planed bellies, as eavesdropped private-seeming things seen through the window from the street

purfling's a sexy word – scroll, end pin, g-string (cuts deep), add d, a, e, and f-holes – ingres, man ray, kiki de montparnasse cut sweet

body parts: peg box, nut and neck to tail-piece; and how to do it: wrist, fingering, shifting position, vibrato, plucked: technique

down – up – down – up – down – the unbuttoned exercises of casanova, paganini, other inabstinents – kreutzer, mazas, maybe (maybe not) sevçik

violin shop on the square, bow rehair and shaved fingerboard ('so worn up there') to help it sing

'long white legs to hand-sized, heart-shaped, incised...' – 'enough', he cries, 'synaesthesic prick-tease'. 'i like it rough', she replies (just as well, considering how he plays) 'darling'

barber's in halifax one saturday night, last buzz-cut gone, lights off, playing le violon de max jaffa – oh some sweet grapelli thing

sweetheart

smart part of town now, full of middle classes who have
moved their arses for the rinky-dink of schools, cafés
(not caffs), touchy-feely global-squeally charity shops
and the pale pink of privilege (as natasha knows,
nigerian princess down the road), what's-yours-is-mine
and plug-in hybrid and (say please) don't scare the ponies.

and there, past some teens flicking through the coat racks (don't look
at theirs, don't stare), maybe five foot three, his childhood sweetie,
it must be, it must be fifty years – more – since they saw
each other, sent a valentine, said 'will you be mine?'
and the mums said 'no' and they had to go and that's that.

this is no mere stare but pools of looks of narcissi
checking each other, checking themselves in each other's
eyes, mirrors, who knows, asking… fuck you cupids: shout out
about saint sebastians har-bloody-pooned with arrows.

it's too late long before the mind stops whirring, unheard
above whatever stuff the skull's stuffed with. time slows, slows –
next time it won't have been for over a century.

the mums succamb to their flames and must be forgiven.
the skies and seas are lovers' eyes, each cloud and tide a doubt.

hold up your hearts to be shriven as lines, words, time runs out.

George Crabbe

'Nature's sternest painter, yet her best'

i
Granny used to say 'don't let me die
in t' workhouse' and I never understood why
until I found she came – her mother came,
ran away after her daddy was killed by a train –
from the winter mud of Suffolk fields to the satanic mills –
different centuries, different worlds (or not). It spills
from the bones – the work, poverty, dna –
into the memory I have of her today.

ii
I first came across him in a big brown leather-bound
book (John Murray, London, 1857) I found
in a second-hand bookshop in Nova Scotia, far
from Aldeburgh's stony beaches and faces, and the vicar
sustained by the restraints of Georgian politer society.
He was in the thesis I didn't finish on English Pastoral Poetry
(that the structure of *The Village* derives from ancient times,
by way of Milton's *Lycidas*); yes, I have sung about Grimes.

iii
Such self-aggrandisement begs the question how much he would care
beyond a kiss for his ununderstanding wife Sarah, and perhaps a rare
treat of slavery-derived sugar in his smuggler-derived tea –
but today we are all guilty, because we know it in the pathetic throes of honesty:
the two eyes for an eye, the gobful for a tooth, the shit in the river
and sea, rapine of the earth and heavens we let be whether or not others live or
die, as long as we don't see them except maybe at 10pm on our 60" tellies,
being bombed by bombs and nursing, like pregnant children, empty bellies.

ta langue

chaque jour je ne pense des enfants
    each day i do not think of the children
chaque jour je ne pense d'amour
    each day i do not think of love
tu ne parle pas ma langue
    you do not speak my language

je voudrais ta langue
    i would like your language
dans ma bouche
    in my mouth
et j'espère que tu aimerais le mien
    and i hope you would like mine

le constructeur m'offre un perroquet vert
    the builder offers me a green parrot
afin de parler les mots
    in order to speak the words
que-est-ce-que tu dit
    what do you say

voilà un hostie de communion
    here is a communion wafer
pour ta langue ta langue
    for your tongue your tongue
dit-moi que-est-ce-que tu dit
    tell me what do you say

demande les perroquets

Animal love song

My person-squirrel nuzzles and nestles and likes a nut.
I never knew a person-aardvark – not as such, but
There was a person-zebra that in its black and white way
Strutted over dreams and honesty while I went grey.
Oh I have been undone by many. Bear. Cougar (once or twice).
Deer (she was, she was). Elephant (we did, you would, nice!)
Fox (oh baby, oh baby). Giraffe (had a laugh – ha!)
This time of year hares, nibbled tips of tall ears the far
Side of the field, while dull bunnies munch on the grass verge.
I could give you more of my bestiary, but the urge
Really diminishes with time. Chuck me an ostrich
Maybe, a tiger, a wolf or a whale, as a bridge
Between your place and mine; or take my hand, be my pet
And, more than person-person, dream me your alphabet.

I want

To hold your hand, to see your smiles,
to carry your love for many [miles].

To make you a cake, to eat yours too,
to talk to you in the bath, and sitting on the [loo].

To be there when you're ill and when you're well,
and let you tell me off when my farts [smell].

Embrace you standing up, and lying on the bed,
and kiss your back and front and arse and [head].

Caress you all the way from head to toe,
and up again until you come, not [go].

Bring flowers and chocs (but I didn't) if I'd been bad
(but I wasn't), so you'd smile when I've left and you're [sad/mad].

When I came back her clothes were gone;
I picked mine off the floor to put them [on].

I can't say where hers was, with whatever hand or smile,
but I carried my love for each and every [mile].

*The square brackets are an
invitation for the reader or
listener to choose rhymes.*

Tuesday afternoon

Is it just my problem, this stick or twist which Waterstones
tries to insist on, sliding tongue and feet into Wetherspoons?
But there again books and beers and beers and books are words
that maybe go together as well as feathers and birds.

And I struggle through Protectorate and Palatinate,
and muddle Palestine and Professor and Procrastinate,
while negotiating the Protesters' (Protestors'?)
tents on King's Parade, on the way to the car via Tesco's.

Complaining in hand-cut rhymes on a sunny Cambridge
day just doesn't quite cut it, bright nylon tents and soft college
walls, cardboard-scrawled signs versus enquiries for teas
and punts, and shouts about Massacrers versus Massacrees.

photograph

exploding fruit – *pow!* – other cartoon words – *splat, spurt* – say
them, see them – if you like (you won't) a trapped ejaculate,
no questions asked about the release of wet sweetness
tasted against the room – a maybe-mouth-agaped caught flight

on the radio the other day someone was talking
about 'smoking', 'smoked', some such, as prison slang for how
he had seen it, how the hole smokes once the bullet has
left it, and how this shows even bad men are given souls now

telly on now the dust no longer rises but leaves a pall,
and it is a pall sanctified on this electric box,
draped over the bombing of faith, hope, charity, and all
the other daily failures of we pretendedly goodly folks

Abduction

Share with me now the dawn of her delight as she walks quietly
    beside the sea, and hears in shells a different world of wind, and storm,
    and possibility.

Broken gulls cut tiny scars on darkening racing skies. A woman as
    man's wealth, with ambered skin and diamond eyes and ruby lips,
    is stolen to be sold for dollars and doubloons, eclipsing blazing suns
    with blackened moons.

They surround and hold her screaming, screaming in the wind. Cuffing
    her cries they grab her, and hold, lift, steal the muffled body in delirious
    cortege aboard their boat.

Borne in water, seas become the air as waves slip faster – clouds grow vast –
    fury strikes in sharp-whipped lightning – thunder furrows, split by crack
    of sail, ripped in the howl of wind and thickening snow – steering goes
    – tiller ploughs uselessly and rudder cannot cut the sea – and at a pole of
    cold and ice the arctic boat bucks to be free of stable world and reined-in
    men, and at extremity a second pole, a second world, screams victory.

Order breaks with sailors' cries – waters roar in mouths and ears
    and eyes – and croaking, unmanned, charnelled men fall fractured
    on a frozen shore.

From a libretto based on Margaret Cavendish's 17th century work The Blazing World

Good wood (wassail)

From acorn to the mighty oak the seed becomes the man,
Until four centuries on the wind destroys the sacred plan.
When we are children oak is green from bud to leaf to love,
But then we're never seen again once we are gone above.

Give good wood to build ships with, and good wood for a chair,
Give good wood sitting all dressed up, and good wood lying bare.

Becoming youth we learn to twine our parts around each other,
Ivy's cling to little deaths in parts incised by lover.
As Jill and Jack we climb the hill to love and live together,
Till Jack and Jill find in the grave their silken skins turned leather.

Give good wood...

The sap has rose to fill the oak, till leaves begin to yellow,
From springtime leap through highest sun to end of life's long mellow.
It bore your branches lovely and bewitched the birds and bees,
From fingers touched by sunny lips to moon toes under trees.

Give good wood...

The oak blows down and breaks its crown, and fills us each with woe,
For green and bud and leaf and love which Jill and Jack forgo.
When life was up the oak blew down, and now is naught but lumber,
Cold log and branch upon the fire burnt hot to ashen slumber.

Give good wood...

The oak was born in springtime, and borne in summer too,
The oak was bared in autumn: I bear winter without you.
Give good wood every morning, and good wood every night,
Give good wood from the dawning to the end of our delight.

Wren and robin (wassail)

The wren is the heart that is held in the height of the sky,
Singing from bush and from branch as the lovers pass by,
Till born is the babe in the end of the year that is gone,
And goes too the weep of the little brown Jenny Wren's song.

With sticks and nets each Stephen's Day
We hunt a wren to steal away (to steal away).
Up with the kettle and down with the pen,
And give us a penny to bury the wren (to bury the wren).

Cock Robin flies up to distract with his sweet melody,
In hark and in lark and in spark from the height of the tree,
But cannot distract with the fire of his breast of red flame
From the truth that the songs of the robin and wren aren't the same.

With sticks and nets...

Jenny is caught in a net on a branch near her nest,
And Cock Robin weeps at her brown flit and flight of distress,
While little babe laughs at the softness of feathers for luck,
Then wails and weeps at the pap when there's nothing to suck.

With sticks and nets...

Father and mother go begging for pennies at doors,
Holding a box for what gift each poor neighbour affords.
So neighbour and friend, for a feather whatever you can,
For fear of the cold little body, and warmth for the cold little man.

With sticks and nets...

Seven coal-heart boys (wassail)

The crows are one, looking with beady eye.
She cries 'take me, take me if you dare' when he comes by.
The crows are two, hung in a leaf-lost tree.
He answers 'make me, make me if you care' and lets her be.

Seven coal-heart boys with wings of blue,
To take the shadows once apart, nor put them back,
To take the shadows once apart, nor change this tune,
Seven coal-heart boys with wings of black.

The crows are three, flocking on frosted land.
She cries 'take me, take me if you dare' and takes his hand.
The crows are four, flapping in dark grey sky.
He answers 'make me, make me if you care' and walks on by.

Seven coal-heart boys...

The crows are five, on roofs sharp as a knife
She cries 'take me, take me if you dare' and takes his life.
The crows are six, a murder that's been done.
He answers 'make me, make me if you care' and is the sun.

Seven coal-heart boys...

The crows are seven, pecking at the end of time.
They cry 'take me, take me if you dare' to fill the rhyme.
The crows are eight as we'll be ate by worm:
They answer 'make me, make me if you care' and don't return.

Seven coal-heart boys...

provocations
(3) the reception of poetry

I

...and there, like a new pair of shoes on a child, is a new poem. Wellies, stilettos (not on a child obviously), sandals or trainers – a poem for any occasion, clean and shiny even if it still pinches and rubs a little (what's that? you wanted the red ones?)

The writer is the child, feeling briefly defined by his or her new pair of shoes, his or her new poem. Power shifts from wearer (writer) to what is worn (poem). The writer is thrilled looking in the mirror, shop windows and other peoples' eyes.

II

Writer and poem are not the same thing. The poem is sent out into a cruel world (the reader's lap, with all that that entails) where it must fend for itself. It must be loud (even if quiet) and proud (even if humble). It is no longer about what the writer may have thought but what others experience unless (and it is a common view) the writer wants to talk about himself or herself in the guise of a poem. A poem needs to work on its own terms and own its own form or it's an indulgence. In that case call it therapy rather than a poem, but yes, they can be the same thing.

III

There are three elements here: Self (writer), Other (reader), and poem (Object). Self communicates to Other through Object. The poem is suspended between writer and reader – does it exist independently of them? – we are in the territory of trees falling down in distant forests. The poem becomes a fact on the page, and is then reformed through being read or heard. It becomes itself through being uncovered, revealed through the archaeology of reading or listening – that is, by an excavation through layers of assumption and prejudice, and of language, form, narrative and emotion.

'Transitional Object' is a term from child development theory to describe a comfort object – for instance a doll, teddy or blanket. Perhaps the same term can be used for some of the rhythms and rhymes and songs that ease us through certain phases of our lives, underpinning and reassuring and focusing our evolving sense of who and how we are.

IV

This is the beginning of the canon. There are two parallel forms of canon: the collective canon of Shakespeare and all the other chaps (they are mainly chaps); and the personal canon. We define ourselves through these two canons, in psychological, social, educational, cultural, gender and generational terms. This splits, in turn, into matters of personal taste, preference and expectation.

There is no such thing as a canonic vacuum. The canon is an issue both for writer and for reader (it will be different for each), with a poem looking nervously between the two. It is integral to our wellbeing – we need, even if we do not want, our children/poems to be versions of ourselves. No, don't shake your head. As readers, the more things conform to these canons the more comfortable we are, even though 'comfort' can contain the need for change (this is why we stay in failing relationships).

Generations feign to overturn but then return to the tropes of the generation before, whether as triumphs or mistakes. I thought our world was triumphing over the horrors of the past but it seems, after all, to be merely trumping them (yes). We write and read while Ukraine and Gaza burn. We tiptoe around whether some things are too big to be subjected to poetry – for example that genocide is the multiplication of the personal.

At least remember that these things are happening and that, by default, we endorse them because we don't oppose them. We vote for other people to endorse them, even by voting for the other other people or by not voting at all. Hypocrisy is cold comfort but, as T S Eliot (quoting Baudelaire) had it, 'Hypocrite lecteur! – mon semblable, - mon frère [et ma soeur]!' To be subject to the collective canon is to be subject to history, and just now history is not repeating itself as farce.

V

Back to basics: here is a poem [insert your choice of poem]. Is it familiar? Is it old or new? I knew poems before I started school – nursery rhymes, Mum's predilection for Edward Lear, Hilaire Beloc, Ogden Nash, A.A.Milne. The canon – my personal canon – was starting to be formed, out of my Mum's background (beyond Hammond Innes and homebrew instructions I have no idea what my father ever read). Here is a silent poem [   ].

VI

The canon relates to development theory as a way in which we broker our relationship with the world – it is an affirmation of identity. A key thing here is the scope of the personal canon to be not a fixed but a changeable thing. To question the canon is the privilege – perhaps the role – of artist and art-lover. To challenge the canon is, arguably, fundamental to the arts as a safe space in which to question. To accept without questioning is complacent, if not dangerous. If the personal canon can evolve, then the collective canon may just shift as well and the world is infinitesimally changed. It is not good enough as it is.

VII

I was told recently about a poet who dismissed all Victorian poetry as 'rubbish'. We have to assume that to your average Victorian with the time, education, money and inclination to read poetry it wasn't all rubbish. With no telly, what else was your average Victorian supposed to do? And the poetry was reacting to what had gone before – those fine young Romantics who lived fast and died young, except for the ones who lived longer and evolved in a haze of High Victorian refulgence into Victorian poets.

We see this with the clinging-on of tonality in music, and the figurative and representational in the visual arts, before their break-down with the cataclysms of the twentieth century. To do poetry justice we need to know how to read the language – not just the words but the worlds around it. There are terms to describe this, with prefixes like socio-psycho-historico-meta- and ending with -ble and -ly.

Look at an old pair of shoes – yours? a child's? on a passer-by? – what does that tell you about the miles walked in them? We may look at the past but we should write and read in relation to the present and the future. Through writing, and through reading and hearing someone's writing, we create something that wasn't there before, and that's amazing.

Janee

This is Janee. Hello Janee.
Janee is six. Janee is quiet.
This is Janee. Janee wears her
Purple tunic for doing ballet.

Janee loves ballet. Janee loves
Mum and Nanna. Janee loves her
Brother and Daddy and two dogs.
They do not all live together.

Janee forgets she has two dogs.
Janee's Nanna speaks no English.
Janee's Nanna sits patiently
Until the dance class is over.

Janee and Nanna go home to
The flat where they live but do not live.
That is somewhere else. Go Janee,
Go, dance like the wind on the Steppes.

Janee asks: 'Nanna, what are the
Steppes?' Nanna nuzzles Janee. We
Could tell them: they are the Pontic-
Caspian Steppes of Eastern Europe.

When Nanna was six there was war there.
Janee is six now: there is war there.
 'Pontic' sounds a bit like what they
Call the Pope. Nanna likes prayers.

If Janee's brother was alive
He would say Americans have
A car called a bit like that. Daddy
Likes cars but drives a tank to work.

Yes the word is like ballet steps
But ballet does not have dead people,
Only in the stories and they
Are made up, aren't they Nanna?

I have made up a story friend
For Janee, who is called Sa'id
And is six. They cannot see each other
Because he can't see and doesn't exist.

Sa'id means 'happy' or 'fortunate'.
Sa'id's Baba was a carpenter,
He hit things with hammers to make them.
Someone said hammers hit people.

Sa'id lives in a different country
But sits side by side here with Janee.
We might call them Janee-Sa'id,
Ha-ha-ha-ha, hee-hee-hee-hee.

Where Janee comes from is a doddle
Really, they only have a few bombs
Most days. Their countries are on TV.
The generations scream silently.

Ghosts

The house seems to have a few mild ghosts, that's all.
John, who was here for years before, said he thought
late evening, once in a while, he could maybe
smell the smell of pipe smoke from some imagined
weary gent leaning by the door, after a
hard day at whatever Victorian men
with few pleasures or pennies did – who like
the house exhaled the woes of centuries in
a final soft fug before the blessèd end.
That thud, that start in the night, may be something
left stupidly aslant by the removals
men that has finally fallen having been
slipping for hours and hours since they left – or he,
the gent, maybe leant on something, knocked it to the
floor with a tipsy hand helped by a bottle
from Mrs Twiddy, on the way to an empty bed.
Or perhaps the smash of dreamt memory, like of
the bastard who at half past two one night after
she died broke into Mum's when I was there,
and I rushed downstairs in fury and the nude –
what the fuck did I think I was going to do?
Or the abuse that seeped like years of leaks
(reminder: must get the plumbing checked)
from someone I trusted, who I have to assume
had been abused too – who talked reverentially,
bizarrely, about the ex-husband and a
'rock 'n' roll lifestyle' like some badge of honour
for, she said, being temporarily blinded.
And so I took her in when she asked, and
the bed was made warm with babies, and time
after time there was white foam in the corners
of her mouth as she yelled past my shoulder.
The chaps ask 'why?': I say 'because I could, I learned
to love, and was blind'. I ask that, taken in
or not, our houses should haunt us merely kindly.

Toccata on 'How'

How they are sat in a dark green Renault Clio
How it is on the King's Road, or no, near the hospital, on the Fulham Road
    just up from the lights
How it is not the Royal Free, the Whittington or St George's Tooting –
    different stories
How you don't know what I'm on about, no you don't, not really
How grandad said he couldn't cope
How a little red matter in a grey cardboard bowl is a lot of red matter
How it is never the right time, and so you have to change concepts of
    rightness and timeness
How it leads to other incontrovertible matters such as love, names and
    school uniforms
How I love the bird song, I think it must be a blackbird that hammers the
    ears with tiny hammers
How it sings now all this is gone, the car is blue and, I don't know why, it
    smells slightly of fish inside

The card

Thanks for the card – that's kind. Touch and go to resist
opening it straightaway but the envelope said
no so I saved it until today. If this reply is
too much, or is not enough, is up to you: I can't say.

Whose offence is the failure to love? Whose offence is
the incapacity to give? By love I think I
mean the capacity to live and let live whoever,
however, whether wankers or saints, we each may be.

The refusal to fight: such arrogance in that but look
how the world isn't helped by anger, how it isn't
healed by lack of trust, abuse, violence, lashing out,
denial, lies: try the weakness of simply turning your back.

And meanwhile others do the fighting for us – handy that,
how we lovers absolve ourselves of responsibility.

missing

not the joyful lean between soft flanks where we
have been but – not dry, it never will be,
because you are too good, but the spooning
intimacies of bed, the talking, breakfasts
(toast, peanut butter) that go with that, and i'll
miss my quiet leer at the normality of
coffee, and nakedness at the foot of the bed

i had in mind to write about someone else,
buried with the indulgence granted a mild
notoriety – she runs off with a poet,
and transmutes her own desires into thickish
words – never mind the sitting or crying, among
the railway stations of the world grand central
does offer a more memorable myth than diss

oh sweetheart, honey, babes (what did he call you?)
were you really smart, to have travelled from the
middle of your huge new world to this remote
little village, slate headstone slipped between
the centuries of neighbours become second
homes, east winds and sodden fields transmuted,
obliterated by idylls of the aga calm (sorry)?

and there is a third beside me saying 'is that
the bird you want to fuck' and we are briefly him
eighteen me sixteen or so and what the fuck does
he know about it, no full breakfasts not even snacks
(though plenty of plums) and him – sorry did i
say eighteen call it eighty – arrested for
the innocence of men – the old ways never fade

promise i will be laid in a peaceful place
like this, or visit if i am already
here by the hedge where the grass thickens and
there are primroses. and whether you take it
forwards or up the arse makes no fucking odds
to any of us, i will still love you and
you will still love me, for as long as we remember

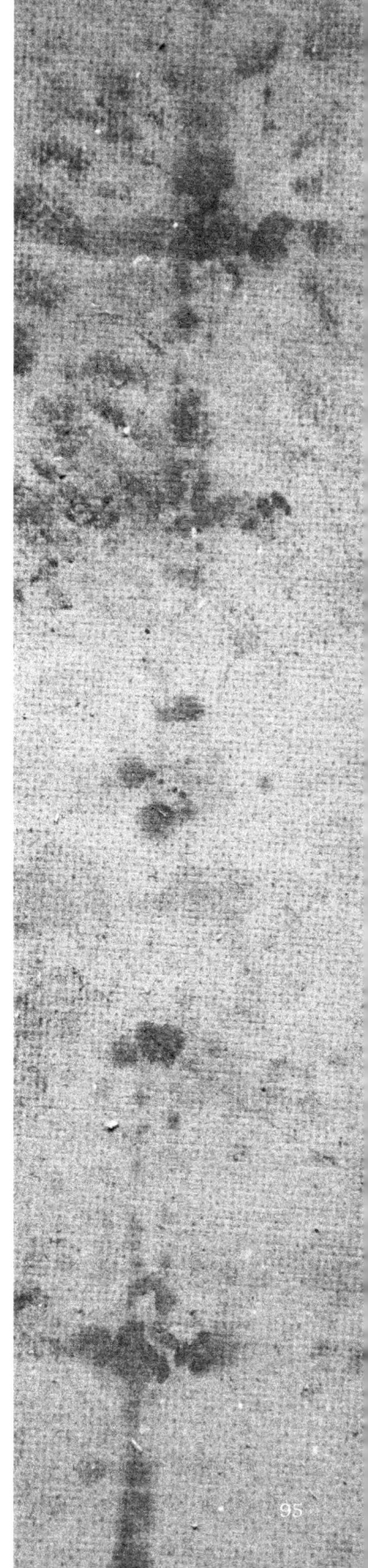

The poet Elizabeth Smart (1913–1986), born in Canada, is best known for her relationship with the poet George Barker and her book By Grand Central Station I Sat Down and Wept. *She is buried in St Cross, South Elmham, Suffolk.*

Autumn

That evening was the first time I had not thought of them
for more than two hours together – a longeur linking
whatever was, and what will necessarily be.

Driving back after, there was one of those sunsets that
should be called 'worldies' or 'goddies' but mainly turn to
dusk, less dove than a pigeon's ungainly grey body.

But fuck me, fuck me you should have seen this evening,
feet in golden fields of stubble and head laced with birds,
such possibilities and echoes of memory.

Other evenings, ordinary ones, cranking the
car door open and glancing up, shadows of new-cut
furrows carved by an old moon thrill me, thrill me baby.

And after conkers large as apples, schools back and mists
at a feeble arm's length, and in bed cat's curves of tongues
and bodies, I do not want to do but do believe in glory.

unicycling on cloud nine

i want to remember what i do not want to forget,
    but i don't know what that is

i want to remember the hole i have just found in my heart,
    because you may have filled it

i want to forget grey eyes and remember brown eyes,
    and how you will laugh so your mouth is larger than the universe

i want to remember brown eyes but i want to forget the search for a word,
    for poetry, to describe them

i want to remember touch that i haven't had,
    and to forget the touches that i have forgotten

i want to remember the maths class that said two positives make a negative
    – or was it two negatives make a positive – i forget

but apart from cream from the supermarket, which I forgot, i remember
    what i want, i think – but i also forgot because i counted on my fingers –
    apples, biscuits, salt, bin bags, there was a fifth for my little finger –
    but i forget, what was it?

the forgotten things are in the past – they are the community speed watch,
    not the mobile police camera, which forgot to forget me

i want to remember to do the things i need to do; i want to forget the things i
    do not want to do – but i must do them

this is the high-wire act (oops), this is cycling along the top of the fence if not
    in the clouds (oops, oops), this is the fear of wanting, the fear of getting,
    and the fear of forgetting (oops, oops, oops)

socks

a lone grey sock crumpled on the floor, a mirror
emptied of its mate, mate absent from its mirror

knuckles brush nipples repeatedly,
a nail is rimed with brown, sweet buttock cupped

two sets of soft edges met in the middle,
he flays her and she is one thrilled bunny

glimpsed past the thick crimps of amputation
where a leg was, on the floor a lone grey sock

*i wanted to know when you would die so i
could love you for ever, but you wouldn't say*

mates absent from their mirrors, mirrors
emptied of their mates, crumpled on the floor

Toccata on 'When'

When someone waves a wand and magicks a peach
When the peach is looking for a fruit bowl
When the fruit bowl next door but one is for sale
When the peach, well, this is not quite what was expected
When it is gently ripened by the sun, and wearing a yellow cardigan, and
    laughs in spite of itself
When words say 'I wanted to know when you would die so I could love you
    for ever' but that was someone else and anyway surely peaches don't
    speak or have ears although this one does
When the peach describes a wire in her chest that sews her cleaved heart
    bones back together
When they said, once upon a time, monks were not allowed peaches because
    they were, well, too peachy
When anyway you do not need to know when someone will die because
    maybe, just maybe, you could love them until after for ever anyway
When someone says 'life's a peach and then you die' and that's better, ah, oh
    my that's better

about

this is a poem about a tree: go outside and see one.

this is a poem about a bird: go outside and hear one.

this is a poem about love: go outside, do it, be it.

this is a poem about a poet: go outside and be one.

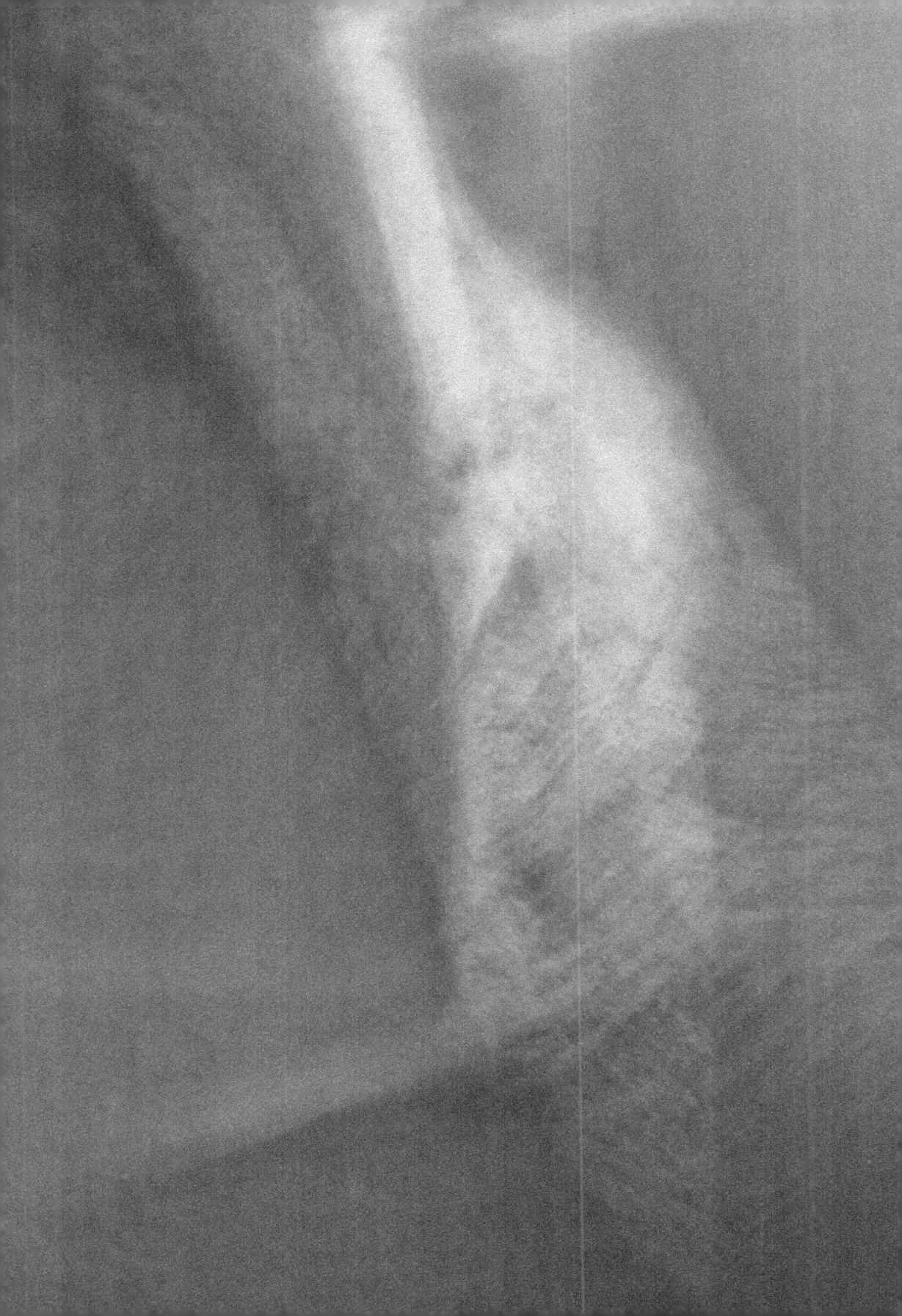

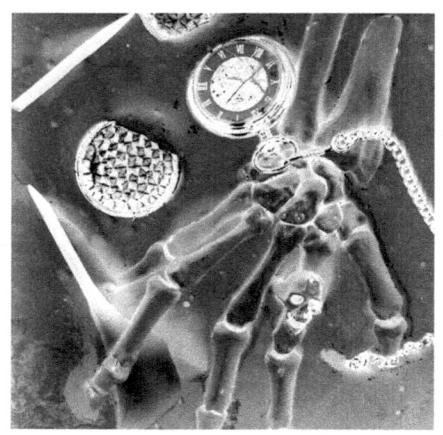

With thanks to Nigel, Paul, John, Jane, Lucy and Melissa

For Francis, Felix and Honor

And for Janee

www.ingramcontent.com/pod-product-compliance
Lightning Source LLC
Chambersburg PA
CBHW061150070526
44584CB00034B/4474